Amazing Quinoa: Family-Friendly Salad, Soup, Breakfast and Dessert Recipes for Better Health and Easy Weight Loss

by Vesela Tabakova

G000067183

Table Of Contents

Why I'm in Love With Quinoa   5
And Now for Its Superfoood Qualities!   5
What Health Conditions Can Eating Quinoa Ameliorate?   7
The Healthiest Way of Cooking Quinoa   9
How to Select and Store   9
Individual Concerns   9
Happy Quinoa Year!   10
Quinoa Salads and Side Dishes   11
Cucumber Quinoa Salad   12
Quinoa and Avocado Salad   13
Quinoa, Blue Cheese and Avocado Salad   14
Italian Chicken Salad with Quinoa   15
Italian Chicken Salad with Quinoa   16
Quinoa Chicken Salad   17
Mashed Avocado, Quinoa and Chicken Salad   18
Fresh Vegetable Quinoa Salad   19
Beetroot Quinoa Salad   20
Quinoa and Black Bean Salad   21
Ham Quinoa Salad   22
Roasted Vegetable Quinoa Salad   23
Quinoa with Oven Roasted Tomatoes and Pesto   24
Quinoa and Feta Stuffed Tomatoes   26
Quinoa Tabbouleh   27
Quinoa, Kale and Roasted Pumpkin   28
Quinoa, Leek and Brussels Sprout Salad   30
Quinoa Salad with Broccoli and Roasted Peppers   31
Quinoa, Zucchini and Chicken Salad   32
Baby Spinach and Quinoa Salad   34
Fresh Mushroom Quinoa Salad   36
Warm Mushroom Quinoa Salad   37
Quinoa Greek Salad   38
Warm Quinoa Salad   39
Quinoa and Asparagus Salad   40
Warm Cauliflower and Quinoa Salad   42
Quinoa, Zucchini and Carrots Salad   43

Quinoa Soups and Main Dishes	44
Red Lentil and Quinoa Soup	45
Spinach, Leek and Quinoa Soup	46
Leek, Quinoa and Potato Soup	47
Vegetable Quinoa Soup	48
Greek Lemon Chicken Soup	49
Chicken Quinoa Soup	50
Lentil, Ground Beef and Quinoa Soup	51
Ground Beef, Quinoa and Brussels Sprouts	52
Stuffed Tomatoes with Quinoa and Ground Beef	53
Beef and Quinoa Meatloaf	55
Mediterranean Chicken and Quinoa Casserole	57
Quinoa and Rosemary Chicken	58
Quinoa Stuffed Bell Peppers	59
Vegetable Quinoa Pilaf	60
Green Pea, Quinoa and Mushroom Stew	62
Curried Quinoa	63
Quinoa and Tomato Stew	64
Spinach and Lentil Quinoa Stew	65
Cabbage Quinoa Stew	66
Quinoa, Leek and Olive Stew	67
Zucchini and Quinoa Stew	68
Quinoa Spinach Stew	69
Vegetable Quinoa Stew	70
Quinoa and Zucchini Fritters	72
Quinoa Breakfasts and Desserts	73
Quinoa Banana Pudding	74
Raisin Quinoa Breakfast	75
Berry Quinoa Breakfast	76
Cherry Quinoa Cookies	77
Quinoa Chocolate Chip Cookies	79
Tahini Quinoa Cookies	80
Quinoa and Banana Muffins	81
Quinoa Fruit Salad	82
Chocolate Quinoa Cake	83
Quinoa Cinnamon Pancakes	85

A Few Words at the End   86
FREE BONUS INSIDE: 20 Healthy Gluten-free Superfood
Smoothies for Easy and Natural Weight Loss   87
Mango and Asparagus Smoothie   88
Pineapple and Asparagus Smoothie   89
Fennel and Kale Smoothie   90
Kids' Favorite Kale Smoothie   91
Kids' Favorite Spinach Smoothie   92
Paleo Mojito Smoothie   93
Winter Greens Smoothie   94
Delicious Kale Smoothie   95
Cherry Smoothie   96
Banana and Coconut Smoothie   97
Avocado and Pineapple Smoothie   98
Carrot and Mango Smoothie   99
Strawberry and Coconut Smoothie   100
Beautiful Skin Smoothie   101
Kiwi and Pear Smoothie   102
Tropical Smoothie   103
Melon Smoothie   104
Healthy Skin Smoothie   105
Paleo Dessert Smoothie   106
Easy Superfood Smoothie   107
About the Author   108

Why I'm in Love With Quinoa

I'm always a little suspicious of anything that gets touted as a 'super-food'. I also try to eat locally grown foods. Which is why it took me a while to get around to trying quinoa. But a few months ago I decided to give it a try. Now all I can say is that I'm in love with quinoa and so glad I discovered this delicious food!

Quinoa is a tiny seed that cooks up like rice and has a mild, nutty flavor and a light, fluffy texture similar to couscous. It turns out that it is not only a super healthy food but is also exceptionally tasty and filling. I think I am getting addicted to experimenting and cooking quinoa in many different ways. Because cooking quinoa is the easiest thing in the world! If you've got 15 minutes, you've got time to cook quinoa.

Just toss some nuts and fruits into boiled quinoa and serve as breakfast porridge. Or include quinoa in casseroles or stews, add it to soups, salads or desserts. I sometimes use sprouted quinoa in salads and sandwiches and even use ground quinoa in breads, cookies, puddings or muffins.

If you haven't tried this amazing food, I highly recommend that you do so. It's extremely inexpensive and full of beneficial nutrients.

And Now for Its Superfoood Qualities!

Famed since ancient Inca times, quinoa has been identified by modern scientists as one of the most nutritious foods in the plant and animal kingdoms. The Incas considered quinoa sacred and called it the "Mother of All Grains". Quinoa is actually the seeds of a plant called goose-foot, which is closely related to spinach, beets and tumbleweeds. It is the only plant food that is gluten free, has a high protein content, and contains all nine essential amino acids.

High quality protein

Quinoa is the only plant-based protein that contains all nine essential amino acids we need for tissue development. These nine essential amino acids are the ones that your body cannot synthesize in quantities sufficient to sustain good health, so they need to come from food sources. There is no disputing the nutritional value of quinoa which enables you to get all of these amino acids from only one product.

Quinoa is rich in linolenic acid, the essential fatty acid that has proven to benefit the body's immune responses.

It is great for babies and young children because of its high content of histadine, the amino acid that is essential to human growth and development.

Recent studies have more great news for quinoa eaters. It seems that the processes of boiling, simmering, and steaming quinoa does not appear to significantly compromise the quality of its fatty acids, allowing us to enjoy its cooked texture and flavor while maintaining this nutrient benefit. Food scientists have speculated that it is the diverse array of antioxidants found in quinoa that contribute to this oxidative protection.

High in fiber and vitamins

Not only high in protein, quinoa is high in fiber, and vitamins such as riboflavin, calcium, vitamin E, iron, potassium, phosphorus, magnesium, folic acid and beta carotene.

Gluten-free

Quinoa is great especially for people who suffer from various conditions due to gluten intolerance as it is completely gluten-free. Not only does it lack gluten but it doesn't even belong to the same plant family as wheat, oats, barley, or rye.

No GMO

Quinoa is nutritionally complex and not genetically modified!

Great for detoxification

Prebiotic nutrients in quinoa help feed the probiotic bacteria in your intestine! The healthier our bacteria, the better chance we have of preventing infections and fighting back disease-causing bacteria.

What Health Conditions Can Eating Quinoa Ameliorate?

Migraine protection

Migraine sufferers can benefit especially from quinoa because its high magnesium and riboflavin content helps prevent the migraine pattern of constricting and rebound dilating of the blood vessels. Migraine sufferers who consume more magnesium in their diets have fewer headaches. Riboflavin's ability to promote cellular energy production has also a beneficial effect on brain and muscle cells metabolism, thus providing further protection against migraine attacks.

Cardiovascular health

People who eat quinoa often will improve their cardiovascular health because of its high magnesium content. Magnesium has proven to help in reducing hypertension, heart arrhythmias and ischemic heart disease because of its ability to relax the blood vessels.

Digestion

Quinoa has proven prebiotic properties. It feeds the beneficial bacteria in our digestive tract. And because it is versatile and easily digested, the body can readily access the vitamins and minerals it contains. Quinoa is also a good source of insoluble fiber, promoting healthy elimination processes, helping maintain colon health and preventing the formation of gallstones.

Detoxifying

The folate and vitamin B in quinoa also boost the liver's ability to eliminate toxins from the body. People at high risk for cancer, as well as those with high blood pressure or cardiovascular disease are often advised to eat more whole grains, yet if they have celiac disease or other forms of gluten sensitivities, they must steer clear of many popular grain products. Quinoa is gluten-free, so those who cannot tolerate gluten can eat it.

Great anti-oxidant

Quinoa offers nearly half the daily minimum requirement for manganese and is a good source of copper and zinc. These minerals are necessary for the synthesis of Super Oxide Dismutase - an enzyme that eliminates free radicals which can cause oxidation damage in the body. Several vitamin companies offer S.O.D. enzyme supplements but quinoa enables your body to produce its own natural enzymes. In that way eating quinoa slows down the effects of aging and helps eliminate cancer cells.

Recent research has also taken a close look at certain antioxidant phytonutrients in quinoa, and two flavonoids — quercetin and kaempferol — are now known to be provided by quinoa in especially concentrated amounts. The concentration of these two flavonoids in quinoa can sometimes be greater than their concentration in high-flavonoid berries like cranberry or lingonberry.

Anti-inflammatory effect

Recent studies are confirming that quinoa seeds are a natural source lots of anti-inflammatory phytonutrients. Their unique combination may be the key to understanding preliminary animal studies that show decreased risk of inflammation-related problems , including obesity, when animals are fed quinoa on a daily basis. The list of anti-inflammatory phytonutrients in quinoa is known to include: polysaccharides; hydroxycinnamic and hydroxybenzoic acids; flavonoids; and saponins including molecules derived from oleanic acid, hederagenin and serjanic acid. Small amounts of the anti-inflammatory omega-3 fatty acid, alpha-linolenic acid (ALA), are also provided by quinoa.

The Healthiest Way of Cooking Quinoa

If you can cook rice, you can cook quinoa. The proportions are the same: two parts liquid to one part quinoa, and so is the method. The only difference is the time. Quinoa only needs to simmer for 15-20 minutes.

To cook quinoa, add one part of the grain to two parts liquid in a saucepan. After the mixture is brought to a boil, reduce the heat to a simmer and cover. Easy – isn't it! One cup of quinoa cooked in this method usually takes 15 minutes to prepare.

When quinoa is ready the grains become translucent, and the white germ has partially detached itself, and looks like a white-spiraled tail.

If you want the quinoa to have an even nuttier flavor, you can dry roast it by placing it in a skillet over medium-low heat and stirring constantly for five minutes. After that you add water, bring it to a boil and follow the same instructions as above.

When quinoa is cooked and ready - cover it and it set aside for 10 minutes.

How to Select and Store

Quinoa is generally available in pre-packaged containers as well as bulk bins. You can usually find it in your local supermarket, but if you don't - look for it at natural foods stores.

Individual Concerns

Quinoa is not a commonly allergenic food and is not known to contain measurable amounts of purines. It is also a gluten-free food. Studies also show a higher-than-expected digestibility for quinoa, making it a food less likely to produce adverse reactions. However, like all members of the chenopodum family, quinoa does contain oxalates, and sometimes in substantial amounts. The oxalate content of quinoa ranges widely, but even the lower end of the oxalate range puts quinoa on the caution or avoidance list for an oxalate-restricted diet.

Although quinoa is gluten free, a few of my recipes are not. If you have gluten intolerance, please always check your ingredients to ensure they do not contain gluten.

Happy Quinoa Year!

The United Nations has declared 2013 the International Year of Quinoa in recognition of the indigenous peoples of the Andes, who have maintained, controlled, protected and preserved quinoa as a food for present and future generations thanks to their traditional knowledge and living practices which are in harmony with nature and Mother Earth.

I hope you enjoy my quinoa recipes and this delicious super food finds an honorable place in your menu!

Quinoa Salads and Side Dishes

Cucumber Quinoa Salad

Serves 6

Ingredients:

1 cup quinoa, rinsed

2 cups water

1 cucumber, peeled and diced

½ cup black olives, pitted and halved

2 tbsp lemon juice

2 tbsp olive oil

1/2 cup finely cut fresh dill

salt and black pepper, to taste

Directions:

Wash quinoa very well in a fine mesh strainer under running water and set aside to drain.

Place quinoa and 2 cups of cold water in a saucepan over high heat and bring to the boil. Reduce heat to low and simmer for 15 minutes.

Set aside, covered, for 10 minutes, then transfer to a large bowl.

Add the finely cut dill, cucumber, and olives.

Prepare a dressing with the lemon juice, olive oil, salt and pepper. Pour it over the salad and gently toss to combine.

Quinoa and Avocado Salad

Serves 4-5

Ingredients:

1 cup quinoa

2 cups water

1 large avocado, peeled and sliced

¼ radicchio, finely sliced

1 small pink grapefruit, peeled and finely cut

a handful of rocket leaves

1 cup baby spinach leaves

2 tbsp olive oil

2 tbsp lemon juice

salt and black pepper, to taste

Directions:

Wash quinoa very well in a fine mesh strainer under running water and set aside to drain.

Place quinoa and 2 cups of cold water in a saucepan over high heat and bring to the boil. Reduce heat to low and simmer for 15 minutes.

Set aside, covered, for 10 minutes, then transfer to a large bowl.

Stir avocado, radicchio, rocket and baby spinach leaves into cooled quinoa. Add in grapefruit, lemon juice and olive oil; season with salt and black pepper, and stir to combine.

Quinoa, Blue Cheese and Avocado Salad

Serves 4-5

Ingredients:

1/2 cup quinoa

1 cup water

1 avocado, peeled and diced

2 tomatoes, diced

1 cup baby spinach, washed and dried

2-3 spring onions, finely chopped

4 oz crumbled blue cheese

2 tbsp lemon juice

2 tbsp olive oil

salt, to taste

Directions:

Wash quinoa very well in a fine mesh strainer under running water and set aside to drain.

Place quinoa and 2 cups of cold water in a saucepan over high heat and bring to the boil. Reduce heat to low and simmer for 15 minutes.

Set aside, covered, for 10 minutes, then transfer to a large bowl.

Stir the baby spinach leaves into cooled quinoa and add in tomatoes, spring onions, avocado and the crumbled blue cheese.

Season to taste with salt, drizzle with lemon juice and olive oil, and toss to combine.

Italian Chicken Salad with Quinoa

Serves 4

Ingredients:

1 cup cooked quinoa

2 roasted or poached chicken breasts, shredded

2 yellow or orange bell peppers, thinly sliced

1 small red onion, thinly sliced

1 medium celery rib, chopped

1/4 cup slivered almonds, toasted

1 tbsp drained capers

juice of one lemon

1 tsp fresh thyme, minced

1/2 cup of Parmesan cheese

1/4 cup olive oil

1 tbsp Dijon mustard

1 tsp sugar

salt and pepper, to taste

Directions:

Combine quinoa, vegetables and chicken in a salad bowl.

Prepare a dressing by mixing the olive oil, lemon juice, mustard, sugar, salt and pepper and pour over the salad.

Stir well to combine and serve.

Italian Chicken Salad with Quinoa

Serves 4

Ingredients:

1 cup cooked quinoa

2 roasted or poached chicken breasts, shredded

2 yellow or orange bell pepper, thinly sliced

1 small red onion, thinly sliced

1 medium celery rib, chopped

1/4 cup slivered almonds, toasted

juice of one lemon

1 tsp fresh thyme, minced

1/2 cup of Parmesan cheese

1/4 cup olive oil

1 tbsp Dijon mustard

1 tsp sugar

salt and pepper, to taste

Directions:

Combine vegetables, chicken and quinoa in a salad bowl.

Prepare a dressing by mixing the olive oil, lemon juice, mustard, sugar, salt and pepper and pour over the salad.

Stir well to combine and serve.

Quinoa Chicken Salad

Serves 5-6

Ingredients:

1 cup quinoa

2 cups water

2 cups chicken breasts, cooked and diced

1 cup green olives, pitted

1 tbsp capers, chopped

1 garlic clove, minced

2 tbsp olive oil

2 tbsp lemon juice

1/2 tsp dried oregano

salt and black pepper, to taste

½ cup finely cut fresh parsley leaves

Directions:

Wash quinoa very well in a fine mesh strainer under running water and set aside to drain.

Place quinoa and 2 cups of cold water in a saucepan over high heat and bring to the boil. Reduce heat to low and simmer for 15 minutes.

Set aside, covered, for 10 minutes, then transfer to a large bowl.

Add in olives, capers, chicken and garlic. Toss to combine.

Prepare the dressing by whisking olive oil, lemon juice, oregano and salt until smooth. Pour it over the salad, toss to combine, and serve sprinkled with fresh parsley.

Mashed Avocado, Quinoa and Chicken Salad

Serves 4

Ingredients:

2 cups cooked chicken breasts, diced

2-3 spring onions, finely chopped

2 ripe avocados, mashed with a fork

1 cup cooked quinoa

1 cup black olives, pitted and chopped

3-4 tbsp lemon juice

3 tbsp olive oil

1 tbsp fresh taragon leaves, finely cut

salt and pepper, to taste

Directions:

Place quinoa, chicken and olives in a salad bowl.

In a plate, mash the avocados using either a fork or a potato masher and add them to the chicken and quinoa.

Add in the onions, taragon, lemon juice and olive oil. Season with salt and black pepper to taste, toss to combine, and serve.

Fresh Vegetable Quinoa Salad

Serves 6

Ingredients:

1 cup quinoa

2 cups water

a bunch of spring onions, chopped

2 green peppers, chopped

½ cup black olives, pitted and chopped

2 tomatoes, diced

1 cup raw sunflower seeds

3 tbsp olive oil

4 tbsp fresh lemon juice

1 tbsp dried mint

Directions:

Prepare the dressing by combining olive oil, lemon juice and dried mint in a small bowl and mixing it well. Place the dressing in the refrigerator until ready to use.

Wash well and cook quinoa according to package directions. When it is ready, leave it aside for 10 minutes, then transfer it to a large salad bowl.

Add the diced peppers, finely cut spring onions, olives and diced tomatoes. Gently toss until vegetables are well combined.

Stir the dressing (it will have separated by this point) and add it to the salad, tossing to evenly coat. Add salt and pepper to taste and sprinkle with sunflower seeds.

Beetroot Quinoa Salad

Serves 4

Ingredients:

½ cup quinoa

1 cup water

2-3 small beets, peeled

3-4 spring onions, finely cut

3 cloves garlic, pressed

2 tbsp red wine vinegar

2-3 tbsp sunflower oil

salt to taste

Directions:

Wash quinoa very well in a fine mesh strainer under running water and set aside to drain.

Place quinoa and 2 cups of cold water in a saucepan over high heat and bring to the boil. Reduce heat to low and simmer for 15 minutes.

Set aside, covered, for 10 minutes, then transfer to a large bowl.

Place the beets in a steam basket set over a pot of boiling water. Steam for about 12-15 minutes, or until tender. Leave to cool.

Grate the beets and add them to the quinoa. Add in the crushed garlic cloves and the finely cut spring onions and stir. Season with salt, vinegar and sunflower oil. Toss to combine and serve.

Quinoa and Black Bean Salad

Serves 6

Ingredients:

1 cup quinoa

1 cup black beans, cooked, rinsed and drained

½ cup sweet corn, cooked

1 red bell pepper, deseeded and chopped

4 spring onions, chopped

1 garlic clove, pressed

1 tbsp dry mint

2 tbsp lemon juice

½ tsp salt

1 tbsp apple cider vinegar

4 tbsp sunflower oil

Directions:

Wash quinoa very well in a fine mesh strainer under running water and set aside to drain.

Place quinoa and 2 cups of cold water in a saucepan over high heat and bring to the boil. Reduce heat to low and simmer for 15 minutes.

Set aside, covered, for 10 minutes, then transfer to a large bowl.

Add in beans, corn, bell pepper, spring onions and garlic. Season with vinegar and black pepper to taste.

In a separate bowl, whisk together lemon juice, salt and sunflower oil and drizzle over the salad. Toss well and serve.

Ham Quinoa Salad

Serves 6

Ingredients:

½ cup quinoa

1 cup water

2 carrots, cooked and diced

½ cup canned green peas, drained

14 oz ham, diced

3-4 pickled gherkins, chopped

½ cup mayonnaise

salt, to taste

Directions:

Rinse quinoa in a fine sieve under cold running water until water runs clear. Strain it and cook it according to package directions. When ready, leave covered for 10 minutes.

Boil carrots, then chop them into small cubes. Chop the ham, the gherkins and put them together with the peas in a salad bowl.

Mix well and stir in quinoa and mayonnaise. Serve cold.

Roasted Vegetable Quinoa Salad

Serves 6

Ingredients:

2 zucchinis, peeled and cut into bite sized pieces

1 eggplant, peeled and cut into bite sized pieces

3 roasted red peppers, cut into bite sized pieces

4-5 small white mushrooms, whole

1 cup quinoa

2 cups water

4 tbsp sunflower oil

3 tbsp olive oil

1 tbsp apple cider vinegar

½ tsp summer savory

7 oz feta, crumbled

Directions:

Toss the zucchinis, mushrooms and eggplant in the sunflower oil, salt and pepper. Place onto a baking sheet in a single layer and bake in a preheated to 390 F oven for 30 minutes flipping once.

Wash well, strain, and cook the quinoa following package directions.

Prepare the dressing by whisking olive oil, apple cider vinegar, savory, salt and pepper until smooth.

In a big bowl, combine quinoa, roasted zucchinis, eggplant, mushrooms, roasted red peppers, and feta. Pour the dressing over the salad and toss to combine.

Quinoa with Oven Roasted Tomatoes and Pesto

Serves 6

Ingredients :

For the salad

1 cup quinoa

2 cups water

1 cup cherry tomatoes, to roast

½ cup cherry tomatoes, fresh

1 avocado, peeled and diced

½ cup black olives, pitted

1 cup mozzarella cheese, cut into bite size pieces

for the pesto

1 clove garlic, chopped

½ tsp salt

½ cup walnuts, toasted

1 cup basil leaves

1 tbsp lemon juice

1 tbsp mustard

4-6 tbsp olive oil

1 tsp summer savory

Directions:

Preheat the oven to 350 F. Line a baking sheet with foil. Wash and pat dry the tomatoes, then drizzle with olive oil and savory and toss to coat them all. Bake the tomatoes for about 20-30 minutes, flipping once, until they are brown. Sprinkle with salt.

Wash quinoa very well in a fine mesh strainer under running water and set aside to drain.

Place quinoa and 2 cups of cold water in a saucepan over high heat and bring to the boil. Reduce heat to low and simmer for 15 minutes.

Set aside, covered, for 10 minutes then fluff with a fork.

Make the pesto by placing the garlic, walnuts and ½ teaspoon salt in a food processor. Add the basil, the mustard and lemon juice and blend in batches until smooth. Add olive oil, one tablespoon at a time, processing in between, until the pesto is light and creamy.

In a large salad bowl, gently mix the quinoa with the roasted and fresh tomatoes, avocado, olives and mozzarella pieces. Add in the pesto and toss to distribute it evenly.

Quinoa and Feta Stuffed Tomatoes

Serves 6

Ingredients:

6 large tomatoes

5.5 oz feta cheese, crumbled

½ cup quinoa

1 cup water

½ cup finely cut fresh parsley

1 tsp paprika

Directions:

Wash and cook quinoa according to package directions. Fluff with a fork and set aside covered.

Cut the top of each tomato in such a way as to be able to stuff the tomato and cover with the cap. Scoop out the seeds and central part of the tomatoes to create a hollow.

Mash the scooped out parts of the tomatoes, add to the feta cheese and stir to make a homogeneous mixture. Add in paprika, parsley and the cooked quinoa.

Stuff the tomatoes with the mixture and cover with the caps. Serve chilled, garnished with sprays of parsley.

Quinoa Tabbouleh

Serves 6

Ingredients:

1/2 cup quinoa

1 cup water

2 cups finely cut parsley

2 tomatoes, chopped

2 garlic cloves, minced

6-7 spring onions, chopped

6-7 fresh mint leaves, chopped

3 tbsp olive oil

juice of one lemon

salt and black pepper, to taste

Directions:

Wash quinoa very well in a fine mesh strainer under running water and set aside to drain.

Place quinoa and 2 cups of cold water in a saucepan over high heat and bring to the boil. Reduce heat to low and simmer for 15 minutes.

Set aside, covered, for 10 minutes.

In a large bowl, mix together the finely cut parsley, tomatoes, olive oil, garlic, spring onions and mint.

Stir in the already chilled quinoa and season to taste with salt, pepper, and lemon juice.

Quinoa, Kale and Roasted Pumpkin

Serves 4-5

Ingredients:

1 cup quinoa

2 cups water

2 cups pumpkin, peeled, seeded, diced

1 cup fresh kale, chopped

1/2 cup crumbled feta cheese

1 small onion, finely chopped

4-5 tbsp olive oil

1 tsp ginger powder

½ tsp cumin

½ tsp salt

Directions:

Preheat oven to 350 F. Line a baking tray and arrange the pumpkin on it. Drizzle with 2-3 tablespoons of olive oil, sprinkle with salt, toss to coat and roast for 15-20 minutes, stirring from time to time.

Heat the remaining olive oil in a large saucepan over medium-high heat. Gently sauté onion, for 2-3 minutes, or until transparent. Add in cumin and ginger powder and cook, stirring, for 1 minute more.

Rinse quinoa very well in a fine mesh strainer under running water; set aside to drain. Place water and quinoa in a large saucepan over medium-high heat. Bring to the boil then reduce heat to low and simmer for 15 minutes. Stir in kale and cook until it wilts.

Gently combine quinoa and kale mixture with the roasted pumpkin and sautéed onion.

Quinoa, Leek and Brussels Sprout Salad

Serves: 5-6

Ingredients:

1 cup quinoa

2 cups water

3 cups Brussels sprouts, halved

1-2 leeks, washed, trimmed and chopped

½ cup almonds, silvered

1 garlic clove, chopped

½ cup fresh dill, finely cut

2 tbsp balsamic vinegar

3 tbsp extra virgin olive oil

Directions:

Preheat the oven to 350 F. Line a baking tray and arrange Brussels sprouts and leeks on it. Drizzle with olive oil, balsamic vinegar and salt and toss to coat. Roast about 20 minutes.

Rinse quinoa very well in a fine mesh strainer under running water; set aside to drain. Place water and quinoa in a large saucepan over medium-high heat.

Bring to the boil then reduce heat to low and simmer for 15 minutes. Remove from heat, fluff with a fork and set aside.

In a salad bowl, toss together the quinoa, Bussels sprouts, leeks, garlic and almonds. Sprinkle with dill, season with salt and pepper to taste, and serve.

Quinoa Salad with Broccoli and Roasted Peppers

Serves: 4

Ingredients:

1 cup quinoa

2 cups vegetable broth

1 small broccoli head, cut into florets

2-3 roasted bell peppers, peeled and chopped

1 small red onion, finely chopped

2 garlic cloves, crushed or chopped

1 tbsp balsamic vinegar

2-3 tbsp olive oil

½ cup fresh dill, finely cut, to serve

salt and black pepper, to taste

Directions:

Wash quinoa very well in a fine mesh strainer under running water and set aside to drain.

Place quinoa and 2 cups of cold water in a saucepan over high heat and bring to the boil. Reduce heat to low and simmer for 15 minutes. Set aside, covered, for 10 minutes.

Arrange broccoli on a baking sheet and drizzle with garlic, olive oil, balsamic vinegar and salt. Toss to coat and roast in a preheated to 350 F oven for about 20 minutes, or until tender.

Transfer the broccoli in a large salad bowl together with the roasted peppers and quinoa. Stir in onion, sprinkle with dill, toss and serve.

Quinoa, Zucchini and Chicken Salad

Serves 4

Ingredients:

1 cup quinoa

2 cups of water

4 chicken breasts, cooked and sliced

1 zucchini, sliced lengthwise into thin ribbons

1 cup cherry tomatoes, halved

5.5 oz feta, crumbled

1 lemon, juice only

4 tbsp olive oil

1 tsp paprika

1 tsp summer savory

1 tsp dried oregano

Directions:

Wash quinoa very well in a fine mesh strainer under running water and set aside to drain.

Place quinoa and 2 cups of cold water in a saucepan over high heat and bring to the boil. Reduce heat to low and simmer for 15 minutes.

Set aside, covered, for 10 minutes.

Place half the olive oil, paprika, savory and oregano in a bowl. Add chicken breasts, season and toss to coat. Place chicken in a pan over medium heat and cook for 4-6 minutes until the skin is golden then turn and cook for a further 6-8 minutes or until ready.

Mix the lemon juice with the remaining olive oil, salt and pepper to taste. In a large bowl, combine the zucchinis, tomatoes, feta and quinoa. Pour over the dressing and stir to combine.

Serve quinoa salad on four plates. Slice the chicken breasts, then arrange on top of the quinoa salad and serve.

Baby Spinach and Quinoa Salad

Serves 6

Ingredients:

½ cup quinoa

1 cup water

½ bag baby spinach, washed and dried

5.5 oz feta cheese, coarsely crumbled

1 red bell pepper, cut in slices

1 cup of cherry tomatoes, halved

1 red onion, finely chopped

1 cup black olives, pitted

1 tsp dried oregano

1 garlic clove, pressed

1/3 cup orange juice

2 tbsp lemon juice

4 tbsp olive oil

salt and black pepper, to taste

Directions:

Wash quinoa with a lot of water. Strain it and cook it according to package directions.

Prepare the dressing by blending garlic, oregano, olive oil, lemon and orange juice in a food processor.

Place the spinach leaves in a large salad bowl and toss with the dressing. Add the rest of the ingredients together with the quinoa and give everything a toss again.

Season to taste with black pepper and salt.

Fresh Mushroom Quinoa Salad

Serves 6

Ingredients:

½ cup quinoa

1 cup water

6 white mushrooms, sliced

1 cup cherry tomatoes, halved

¼ cup walnuts, chopped

½ cup finely cut fresh parsley

3-4 spring onions, finely cut

½ cup black olives, pitted and halved

for the dressing:

2 tbsp orange juice

1 tbsp apple cider vinegar

2 small garlic cloves, minced

2 tbsp olive oil

salt and black pepper, to taste

Directions:

Wash quinoa with a lot of water. Strain it and cook it according to package directions. Cover and allow to cool for 10 minutes.

Combine mushrooms, tomatoes, onions, olives, parsley and walnuts in a large bowl. Add the already cooled quinoa.

Whisk together the dressing ingredients and toss with the salad just before serving.

Warm Mushroom Quinoa Salad

Serves 4-5

Ingredients:

1 cup quinoa

2 cups vegetable broth

1 tbsp sunflower oil

2-3 spring onions, chopped

2 garlic cloves, chopped

10 white mushrooms, sliced

1-2 springs of fresh rosemary, leaves only

½ cup oil-packed sun-dried tomatoes, chopped

2 tbsp olive oil

salt and black pepper, to taste

½ cup fresh parsley, finely cut, to serve

Directions:

Wash well the quinoa in plenty of cold water, strain it and put it in a saucepan. Add vegetable broth and bring to the boil. Lower heat and simmer for 10 minutes until the broth is absorbed.

Heat olive oil in a frying pan and sauté onions for 2-3 minutes; add the garlic and sauté for another minute. Add sliced mushrooms and season with salt and pepper. Finally, add the rosemary. Stir-fry the mushrooms until soft.

Mix well the cooked quinoa with the mushrooms and sun-dried tomatoes. Serve sprinkled with fresh parsley.

Quinoa Greek Salad

Serves 6

Ingredients:

1 cup quinoa

2 cups water

1 red pepper, diced

1 green pepper, diced

1 cucumber, diced

½ cup black olives, pitted

1 small red onion, diced

5.5 oz feta cheese, crumbled

2 tbsp olive oil

2 tbsp lemon juice

2-3 fresh basil leaves

black pepper, to taste

Directions:

Wash well the quinoa in plenty of cold water, strain it and put it in a saucepan. Add water and bring to the boil. Lower heat and simmer for 10 minutes, or until the water is absorbed. Set aside to cool.

Stir vegetables and crumbled feta cheese into quinoa. Prepare the dressing by whisking together olive oil, lemon juice, garlic, basil, salt and pepper. Pour over quinoa mixture and toss to combine.

Warm Quinoa Salad

Serves 6

Ingredients:

1 cup quinoa

2 cups of water

½ cup green beans, frozen

½ cup sweet corn, frozen

½ cup carrots, diced

½ cup black olives, pitted

2 garlic cloves, pressed

3-4 tbsp soy sauce

2-3 tbsp lemon juice

2 tbsp olive oil

salt and black pepper, to taste

Directions:

Wash quinoa with a lot of water. Strain it and cook it in two cups of water for 15 minutes. When ready, set aside in a large salad bowl.

Gently stew the green beans, sweet corn and carrots in a little olive oil for 5-10 minutes or until tender then add to the quinoa.

In a smaller bowl or cup, combine soy sauce, lemon juice and garlic and pour over the warm salad. Add salt and pepper to taste and serve.

Quinoa and Asparagus Salad

Serves 6

Ingredients:

1 cup quinoa, rinsed

2 cups water

8-9 spears of asparagus, woody ends trimmed, cut

2 bell peppers, deseeded, chopped

5.5 oz feta cheese, crumbled

¼ cup raw sunflower seeds

4 spring onions, chopped

2 tbsp fresh parsley, finely cut

2 tbsp lemon juice

1 tbsp honey

2 tbsp olive oil

1 tsp paprika

black pepper, to taste

Directions:

Wash quinoa very well in a fine mesh strainer under running water and set aside to drain.

Place quinoa and 2 cups of cold water in a saucepan over high heat and bring to the boil. Reduce heat to low and simmer for 15 minutes.

Set aside, covered, for 10 minutes.

Preheat a grill pan and cook the asparagus for 2-3 minutes, or until tender crisp. Combine it with the bell peppers, feta cheese, sunflower seeds, spring onions, parsley and quinoa.

Whisk the lemon juice, honey, olive oil and paprika in a small bowl until well combined. Add the dressing to the quinoa mixture. Season with black pepper and toss to combine.

Warm Cauliflower and Quinoa Salad

Serves 4

Ingredients:

1/2 cauliflower, cut into florets

1 cup quinoa

2 cups water

1 tsp paprika

5-6 spring onions, finely cut

5-6 small mozzarella cheeses, halved

5-6 tbsp olive oil

Directions:

Preheat oven to 390 F. Cut cauliflower into bite sized pieces. Place it in a roasting dish and toss in olive oil and paprika. Roast, stirring occasionally, until the cauliflower is golden on the edges and soft.

Wash quinoa well and place in a medium saucepan with two cups of water. Simmer for 15 minutes then set aside for 3-4 minutes to cool.

Serve quinoa topped with cauliflower and sprinkled with cheese and spring onions.

Quinoa, Zucchini and Carrots Salad

Serves 6

Ingredients:

1 cup quinoa

2 cups water

2 big carrots, sliced lengthwise into thin ribbons

1 zucchini, sliced lengthwise into thin ribbons

1 big cucumber, peeled and sliced lengthwise into thin ribbons

2 garlic cloves, pressed

2 tbsp orange juice

1 tbsp apple cider vinegar

1 tbsp honey

2 tbsp olive oil

Directions:

Wash quinoa very well in a fine mesh strainer under running water and set aside to drain.

Place quinoa and 2 cups of cold water in a saucepan over high heat and bring to the boil. Reduce heat to low and simmer for 15 minutes. Set aside, covered, for 10 minutes.

Peel lengthwise the carrots and zucchini into thin ribbons. Steam them for 3-4 minutes. Peel the cucumber into ribbons too.

Prepare a dressing by mixing the orange juice, vinegar, honey, olive oil and garlic.

Serve quinoa on each plate and arrange some of the vegetable stripes over it. Top with 2-3 tablespoons of the dressing and serve.

Quinoa Soups and Main Dishes

Red Lentil and Quinoa Soup

Serves 4-5

Ingredients:

½ cup quinoa

1 cup red lentils

5 cups water

1 onion, chopped

2-3 garlic cloves, chopped

1 red bell pepper, finely cut

1 small tomato, chopped

3 tbsp olive oil

1 tsp ginger

1 tsp cummin

1 tbsp paprika

salt and black pepper, to taste

Directions:

Rinse quinoa and lentils very well in a fine mesh strainer under running water and set aside to drain.

In a large soup pot, heat the olive oil over medium heat. Add the onion, garlic and red pepper and sauté for 1-2 minutes until just fragrant. Stir in paprika, spices, red lentils and quinoa.

Add in water and gently bring to a boil then lower heat and simmer, covered, for 30 minutes. Add the chopped tomato and salt and cook for 5 minutes more. Blend the soup and serve.

Spinach, Leek and Quinoa Soup

Serves 6

Ingredients:

½ cup quinoa

2 leeks, halved lengthwise and sliced

1 onion, chopped

2 garlic cloves, chopped

1 can tomatoes, diced, undrained

2 cups of fresh spinach leaves, cut

2 cups vegetable broth

3 cups water

2 tbsp sunflower oil

1 tsp paprika

salt and pepper, to taste

3-4 tbsp lemon juice, to serve

Directions:

Heat a large soup pot over medium heat. Add oil and onion and sauté for 2 minutes. Add in leeks and cook for another 2-3 minutes, then add garlic and paprika and stir. Season with salt and black pepper to taste.

Add the vegetable broth, water, canned tomatoes, and quinoa.

Bring the soup to a boil then reduce heat and simmer for 15 minutes. Stir in the spinach and cook for another 5 minutes. Serve with lemon juice.

Leek, Quinoa and Potato Soup

Serves 6

Ingredients:

½ cup quinoa

4 cups water

2-3 potatoes, diced

1 small onion, cut

1 leek, halved lengthwise and sliced

3 tbsp olive oil

lemon juice, to taste

Directions:

Heat a soup pot over medium heat. Add olive oil and onion and sauté for 2 minutes. Add in leeks and potatoes, stir, and cook for a few minutes more.

Add water, bring to a boil, reduce heat and simmer for 5 minutes. Add in the very well washed quinoa and simmer for 10 minutes. Serve with lemon juice to taste.

Vegetable Quinoa Soup

Serves 6

Ingredients:

½ cup quinoa

1 onion, chopped

1 potato, diced

1 carrot, diced

1 red bell pepper, chopped

2 tomatoes, chopped

1 zucchini, diced

4-5 cups water

1 tsp paprika

1 tsp summer savory

3-4 tbsp olive oil

2 tbsp fresh lemon juice

Directions:

Rinse quinoa very well in a fine mesh strainer under running water and set aside to drain.

Heat the oil in a large soup pot and gently sauté the onions and carrot for 2-3 minutes, stirring every now and then. Add paprika, savory, potato, bell pepper, tomatoes and water. Stir to combine.

Cover, bring to a boil, then lower heat and simmer for 10 minutes. Add in the quinoa and zucchini; stir, cover and simmer for 15 minutes, or until the vegetables are tender. Add in the lemon juice; stir to combine and serve.

Greek Lemon Chicken Soup

Serves 4-5

Ingredients:

1.2 oz uncooked boneless, skinless chicken breast, diced

1/3 cup quinoa

3 cups chicken broth

1 cup water

1 onion, finely diced

2 raw eggs

3 tbsp olive oil

1/2 cup fresh lemon juice

1 tsp salt

1/2 tsp ground black pepper

1/2 cup finely cut parsley, to serve

Directions:

In a medium pot, heat the olive oil and sauté the onions until they are soft and translucent. Add in chicken broth, water, diced chicken and washed quinoa.

Bring to a boil, reduce heat and simmer for 20 minutes or until the chicken is cooked through.

In a small bowl, beat the eggs and lemon juice together. Pour two cups of broth slowly into the egg mixture, whisking constantly. When all the broth is incorporated, add this mixture back into the pot of chicken soup and stir well to blend. Do not boil any more.

Season with salt and pepper and garnish with parsley. Serve hot.

Chicken Quinoa Soup

Serves 4

Ingredients:

2 chicken breasts

1 onion, chopped

2 cloves garlic, chopped

1 celery rib, chopped

1-2 carrots, cut

1 tsp paprika

1 bay leaf

1/2 cup quinoa, rinsed

3 cups chicken broth

2 cups water

salt and pepper, to taste

lemon juice, to serve

Directions:

Heat olive oil in a large soup pot and gently sauté onions, carrots, celery and garlic. Add in broth, water, the chicken breasts and bring to the boil. Reduce heat and simmer slowly until cooked through.

Remove chicken, cut it in cubes and set aside in a bowl. Add quinoa to the soup and simmer for 10 minutes, then return the chicken and serve.

Lentil, Ground Beef and Quinoa Soup

Serves 4-5

Ingredients:

1 lb ground beef

1/2 cup quinoa

1/1 cup green lentils

1 carrot, chopped

1 onion, chopped

1 small potato, peeled and diced

2-3 garlic cloves, chopped

2 tomatoes, grated or pureed

5 cups water

1 tsp summer savory or dried mint

1 tsp paprika

2 tbsp olive oil

1 tsp salt

ground black pepper, to taste

Directions:

Heat olive oil in a large soup pot. Brown the ground beef, breaking it up with a spoon. Add in paprika and garlic and stir. Add lentils, washed quinoa, remaining vegetables, water and spice.

Bring the soup to a boil. Reduce heat to low and simmer, covered, for about 40 minutes, or until the lentils are tender. Stir occasionally.

Ground Beef, Quinoa and Brussels Sprouts

Serves: 4

Ingredients:

6 oz ground beef

1/2 small onion, finely cut

2 garlic cloves, crushed

1/2 cup quinoa

1 cup water

½ cup grated sweet potato

1 cup grated Brussels sprouts

1 tbsp olive oil

Directions:

In a saucepan, heat the olive oil over medium heat. Gently saute the onion and garlic until fragrant. Add in the ground beef, sweet potato and quinoa and stir.

Add the water and bring to a boil then simmer for 20 minutes or until the meat is fully cooked.

Stir in the Brussels sprouts and cook for 5-6 minutes more. Season with salt and pepper to taste and serve.

Stuffed Tomatoes with Quinoa and Ground Beef

Serves 6

Ingredients:

1 lb ground beef

6 large tomatoes

2 tbsp tomato paste or purée

1/2 cup quinoa

1 onion, shredded

2 garlic cloves, crushed

6 tsp sugar

1 tsp paprika

1 tsp mint

1/2 cup parsley leaves, finely cut

5 tbsp olive oil

salt and pepper, to taste

2/3 cup Parmesan cheese, grated

Directions:

Slice the tops of the tomatoes in such a way as to be able to stuff the tomato and cover with the cap. With the help of a spoon, scoop out the tomato flesh and reserve in a bowl. Sprinkle a teaspoon of sugar in each tomato to help reduce the acidity.

Heat the olive oil in a large skillet and brown the ground beef. Add in the onion and garlic and cook until transparent. Add the very well washed quinoa, parsley, finely cut tomato pulp and tomato paste. Season with paprika, mint, salt and pepper. Bring to the boil, then reduce heat and simmer for 5 minutes.

Drizzle some olive oil in the bottom of an ovenproof casserole. Arrange the tomatoes in the dish. Stuff them with the beef and quinoa mixture - each tomato should be about 3/4 full.

Sprinkle with Parmesan cheese and bake in a preheated to 350 F oven for 30 minutes.

Beef and Quinoa Meatloaf

Serves 4

Ingredients:

1/2 cup quinoa

1 cup water

1 small red onion, grated

1 lb ground beef

1 carrot, peeled, grated

3 oz feta cheese, crumbled

2 tbsp tomato sauce

1 egg, lightly beaten

2 tbsp basil leaves, finely cut

1 zucchini, thinly sliced

1 cup cherry tomatoes

1 garlic clove, crushed

2-3 tbsp olive oil

Directions:

Cook quinoa following package directions. Set aside to cool.

Preheat oven to 350 F. Grease base and sides of a 8 x 4 x 2.5 inch loaf pan or line it with baking paper, allowing a 1 inch overhang at both long ends.

Combine quinoa, onion, ground beef, carrot, feta, sauce, egg and basil in a bowl. Mix well and press into prepared pan.

Place the zucchini, tomatoes and garlic in a bowl. Toss in olive oil. Arrange over meatloaf.

Bake for 40-50 minutes or until the meatloaf is firm. Set aside for 10 minutes, slice and serve.

Mediterranean Chicken and Quinoa Casserole

Serves 4

Ingredients:

1/2 cup quinoa

4 chicken breast halves

1 onion, sliced

1 red bell pepper, thinly sliced

2 cups tomato pasta sauce

1/2 cup black olives, pitted

1/2 green olives, pitted

1/3 cup Parmesan cheese

¼ cup chopped parsley

3 tbsp olive oil

Directions:

Heat the oil in a large, deep frying pan over medium-high heat. Cook chicken breasts, turning, for 4 to 5 minutes or until golden. Transfer to a casserole.

Sauté the onion and bell pepper, stirring, for 3 to 4 minutes, or until the onion has softened. Transfer to the casserole. Add in well washed quinoa, pasta sauce and olives.

Season with salt and pepper and bake in a preheated to 350 F for 30-35 minutes, stirring several times. Sprinkle with Parmesan cheese and parsley and bake for 3-4 minutes more.

Quinoa and Rosemary Chicken

Serves 4

Ingredients:

4 boneless skinless chicken breasts, diced

1/2 cup quinoa

1 cup chicken broth

2 garlic cloves, crushed

1 tbsp capers

1 tbsp dried rosemary

3 tbsp olive oil

salt and pepper, to taste

Directions:

Heat olive oil in a skillet over medium-low heat and sauté the garlic for about a minute. Add in the chicken pieces and cook for 2-3 minutes, stirring.

Add in rosemary, capers, salt and pepper to taste, quinoa and chicken broth. Stir, cover, and cook, on medium-low, for 20 minutes or until the chicken is cooked through.

Quinoa Stuffed Bell Peppers

Serves 6

Ingredients:

8 red or green bell peppers, cored and seeded

1 cup quinoa

2 cups water

1 onion, chopped

1 tomato, chopped

a bunch of fresh parsley, chopped

3 tbsp olive oil

1 tbsp paprika

Directions:

Heat the oil and sauté the onion for 2-3 minutes. Add in paprika, the washed and rinsed quinoa and the chopped tomato. Season with salt and pepper. Add in one cup of hot water and cook quinoa until the water is absorbed.

Stuff each pepper with the mixture using a spoon. Every pepper should be ¾ full.

Arrange the peppers in a deep ovenproof dish and top up with warm water to half fill the dish. Cover and bake for about 10 minutes at 350 F. Uncover and cook for another 5 minutes or until the peppers are well cooked.

Vegetable Quinoa Pilaf

Serves 6

Ingredients:

1 cup quinoa

2 cups water

1 red bell pepper, chopped

1 small eggplant, chopped

1 zucchini, chopped

2 spring onions, thinly sliced

2 garlic cloves, cut

1 tsp summer savory

1 tsp dried oregano

3 tbsp olive oil

3 tbsp lemon juice

salt and pepper, to taste

Directions:

Wash quinoa very well in a fine mesh strainer under running water and set aside to drain.

Place quinoa and 2 cups of cold water in a saucepan over high heat and bring to the boil. Reduce heat to low and simmer for 15 minutes.

Set aside, covered, for 10 minutes.

Heat olive oil in a heavy based saucepan over medium-high heat. Add the bell pepper, eggplant and onions. Sauté, stirring, for 2 minutes then cover and cook for 10 more minutes.

Add in the zucchini, garlic, savory and oregano and toss to combine. Cook until the zucchini is tender.

Add lemon juice and quinoa. Season with salt and pepper to taste, stir to combine, and serve sprinkled with parsley.

Green Pea, Quinoa and Mushroom Stew

Serves 4

Ingredients:

1 cup green peas (fresh or frozen)

1 cup quinoa

4-5 large white button mushrooms, sliced

3 green onions, chopped

1 big carrot, chopped

1-2 cloves garlic

2 cups vegetable broth

4 tbsp sunflower oil

1/2 cup water

1/2 cup finely chopped dill

salt and black pepper, to taste

Directions:

In a saucepan, sauté mushrooms, carrot, green onions and garlic.

Add in green peas, very well washed quinoa, vegetable broth and bring to a boil.

Lower heat and simmer for 15 minutes. Sprinkle with dill and serve.

Curried Quinoa

Serves 4

Ingredients:

1 cup quinoa

3 green onions, chopped

1 big carrot, chopped

1-2 cloves garlic

2 cups vegetable broth

3 tbsp sunflower oil

1 tbsp curry powder, or to taste

salt and black pepper, to taste

Directions:

Heat oil in a large skillet over medium heat. Add in onions, garlic and carrot and cook for 2 minutes, stirring.

Stir in very well washed quinoa and vegetable broth and bring to a boil. Lower heat, add curry powder and simmer for 15 minutes.

Season to taste with salt and pepper, and serve.

Quinoa and Tomato Stew

Serves 6-7

Ingredients:

1 cup quinoa

2 cups water

1 big onion, chopped

1 carrot, chopped

2 cups tomatoes, diced or from a can

3-4 tbsp olive oil

1 tsp summer savory

1 tsp paprika

½ cup finely cut fresh parsley

1 tsp sugar

Directions:

Wash and drain quinoa. In a large saucepan, sauté the onion and carrot in olive oil for 4-5 minutes.

Add in paprika and stir. Add in water and tomatoes. Stir well to combine and season with salt, pepper, savory and a teaspoon of sugar to neutralize the acidic taste of the tomatoes. Bring to the boil and add in quinoa.

Reduce heat and simmer for about 25 minutes. When all liquid has evaporated, sprinkle with parsley and serve.

Spinach and Lentil Quinoa Stew

Serves 5-6

Ingredients:

1/2 cup brown lentils

1/2 cup quinoa

3 cups fresh spinach or about half package of frozen spinach, thawed

1 onion, chopped

2 medium carrots, chopped

2 cloves garlic, cut

3 tbsp olive oil

1 tsp paprika

1 tbsp summer savory

3 cups water

salt and pepper, to taste

Directions:

Heath olive oil in a big saucepan and sauté the onion and carrots for 4-5 minutes, stirring. Add in garlic, paprika, savory and lentils and sauté for a minute until just fragrant. Add in water, bring to a boil, lower the heat and cook for 15 minutes.

Rinse the quinoa and add it to the pot with salt and pepper to taste. Stir well and bring to the boil then lower heat and simmer for 10 minutes.

Cut the spinach and add it to the pot. Cook for 4-5 more minutes or until it wilts.

Cabbage Quinoa Stew

Serves 5-6

Ingredients:

1 cup quinoa

2 cups water

1 small onion, chopped

1 garlic clove, pressed

¼ head cabbage, cored and shredded

2 tomatoes, diced

2 tbsp olive oil

1 tbsp paprika

½ cup finely cut fresh parsley

salt to taste

black pepper, to taste

Directions:

Heat the olive oil in a large pot. Add the onion and garlic and cook until transparent. Add the paprika and the shredded cabbage and cook, stirring, for 2-3 minutes. Add water, cover, and simmer for 10 more minutes.

Wash quinoa and add it to the pot together with the tomatoes. Simmer for about 15 minutes, stirring occasionally, until the liquid is absorbed.

Season with salt and pepper and set aside for 10 minutes. Serve sprinkled with parsley.

Quinoa, Leek and Olive Stew

Serves 4-6

Ingredients:

6-7 cups of sliced leeks

1 medium onion, chopped

20 black olives, pitted and halved

1 cup quinoa

2 ½ cups water

3-4 tbsp olive oil

salt and black pepper, to taste

Directions:

In a large saucepan, sauté the leeks and onion in the olive oil for 4-5 minutes. Cut and add the olives and 1/2 cup water. Lower heat, cover saucepan and cook for 10 minutes, stirring occasionally.

Add in the well washed quinoa with 2 cups of warm water. Bring to a boil, cover, and simmer for 15 more minutes, stirring occasionally.

Remove from heat and allow to 'sit' for 10 minutes before serving.

Zucchini and Quinoa Stew

Serves 5-6

Ingredients:

1 cup quinoa

2 cups water

3-4 small zucchinis, diced

2 medium tomatoes, diced

1 bunch of spring onions, finely chopped

1 bunch of fresh dill, finely cut

3 tbsp olive oil

1 tsp salt

1 tsp paprika

1/2 tsp black pepper

Directions:

In a large saucepan, sauté spring onions in olive oil and a little water. Add zucchinis and tomatoes and cook for 5 minutes.

Add in paprika, quinoa, finely cut dill and 2 cups of warm water. Bring to the boil, reduce heat, cover, and simmer for 15-20 minutes.

Quinoa Spinach Stew

Serves 4

Ingredients:

1.5 lb fresh spinach, washed, drained and chopped

1 cup quinoa

2 cups water

1 onion, chopped

1 tomato, diced

1 carrot, chopped

3 tbsp olive oil

1 tbsp paprika

salt and black pepper, to taste

Directions:

Heat the oil in a large saucepan and sauté the onions and carrot until tender. Add paprika and the spinach leaves. Stir and add in the diced tomato and two cups of warm water.

Bring to the boil, add the well washed quinoa, stir, cover and and simmer for 10 minutes.

Remove from the heat, season to taste and set aside for 10 minutes. Serve warm or room temperature.

Vegetable Quinoa Stew

Serves 6-7

Ingredients:

1 cup quinoa

2 cups water

1 onion, finely cut

2 potatoes, peeled and diced

2 tomatoes, diced

1 carrot, cut

½ cup frozen peas

½ cup frozen green beans

1 zucchini, peeled and diced

1 red bell pepper, cut

2-3 garlic cloves, cut

4 tbsp olive oil

salt and pepper, to taste

1 tbsp paprika

1 cup finely cut fresh parsley

Directions:

In a deep saucepan, heat olive oil and sauté the onion and carrot for a few minutes. Add in garlic, green peas, green beans, potatoes, zucchini and bell pepper and sauté, stirring, for a few more minutes.

Reduce heat, cover, and cook stirring occasionally, until

vegetables soften. Add in paprika, tomatoes, parsley and quinoa and continue to simmer for 15 more minutes.

Quinoa and Zucchini Fritters

Serves 4

Ingredients:

3 zucchinis, peeled and grated

4 eggs

1 cup cooked quinoa

1/2 cup fresh dill, finely cut

1 tsp fresh mint, chopped

3 garlic cloves, crushed

5-6 spring onions, very finely chopped

1 cup feta cheese, crumbled

salt and black pepper, to taste

1/2 cup sunflower oil, for frying

Directions:

Grate zucchinis and put them in a colander. Sprinkle with salt set aside to drain for 15 minutes. Squeeze and place in a bowl. Add in quinoa and all other ingredients except for the sunflower oil. Stir very well.

Heat the sunflower oil in a frying pan. Drop a few scoops of the zucchini quinoa mixture and fry them on medium heat, making sure they don't touch.

Fry for 3-5 minutes, until golden brown. Serve with yogurt.

Quinoa Breakfasts and Desserts

Quinoa Banana Pudding

Serves 4

Ingredients:

1 cup quinoa

2 cups water

3 ripe bananas

3 cups milk

4 tbsp sugar

1 tsp vanilla extract

Directions:

Wash and cook quinoa according to package directions. When ready remove from heat and set aside.

In a separate bowl blend sugar, milk and bananas until smooth. Add to the quinoa.

Heat over medium heat, string, until creamy. Stir in vanilla and serve warm.

Raisin Quinoa Breakfast

Serves 2

Ingredients:

½ cup quinoa

1 cup milk

2-3 tbsp honey, optional

1 tsp cinnamon

½ tsp vanilla

½ tsp ground flaxseed

2 tbsp walnuts or almonds, chopped

2 tbsp raisins

Directions:

Rinse quinoa and drain. Place milk and quinoa into a small saucepan and bring to a boil.

Add cinnamon and vanilla.

Reduce heat to low and simmer for about 15 minutes, stirring often.

When ready, place a portion of the quinoa into a bowl, drizzle with honey and top with flax seeds, raisins and crushed walnuts.

Berry Quinoa Breakfast

Serves 2

Ingredients:

½ cup quinoa

1 cup milk

¼ cup fresh blueberries or raspberries

1 tbsp walnuts or almonds, chopped

Directions:

Wash quinoa and cook according to package directions. Combine it with milk in and bring to a boil.

Cover, reduce heat and simmer for 15 minutes.

When ready add walnuts and cinnamon, place a portion of the quinoa into a bowl and top with fresh blueberries.

Cherry Quinoa Cookies

Serves 10-12

Ingredients:

1 cup cooked quinoa

1 cup whole wheat flour

4 tbsp unsalted butter, melted

¼ cup honey

¼ cup sugar

½ cup dried cherries

boiling water

½ tsp baking powder

½ tsp salt

1 egg

1 tsp vanilla extract

½ cup sliced almonds or walnuts

Directions:

Soak dried cherries in boiling water for 10 minutes then strain and set aside.

In a medium bowl, whisk together flour, baking powder, and salt.

In a large bowl, whisk together butter, honey and sugar until well combined and lightened in color. Whisk in the egg. Add vanilla extract and beat again.

Stir in flour mixture, quinoa, almonds, and cherries until well combined. Cover dough and let "sit" for half an hour.

Preheat oven to 350 F. Line two baking sheets with baking paper. Place a teaspoon of cookie dough into the palm of your hand. Roll it between your palms until it becomes spherical.

Align every cookie dough about 2 inch from the previous. Bake cookies until golden, about 12 minutes.

Quinoa Chocolate Chip Cookies

Serves 10

Ingredients

1 cup quinoa

1 cup flour

½ cup of melted butter

½ cup sugar

1 egg

½ tsp baking powder

½ tsp salt

1 tsp vanilla powder

5.5 oz chocolate chips

Directions:

Cream butter and sugar together. Add eggs and vanilla and beat some more.

Mix dry ingredients together separately then slowly add them to the butter mixture. Add the chocolate chips.

Preheat oven to 350 F. Line two baking sheets with baking paper. Place a teaspoon of cookie dough into the palm of your hand. Roll the cookie dough between your palms until it retains a spherical shape.

Align every cookie dough about 2 inch from the previous. Bake cookies until golden, about 12 minutes.

Tahini Quinoa Cookies

Serves 8-10

Ingredients:

1 cup rice flour

1 cup quinoa

½ cup honey

1/3 cup brown sugar

½ cup butter

½ cup tahini

1 tsp baking soda

¼ tsp salt

½ teaspoon vanilla

Directions:

Preheat oven to 350 F degrees. Combine sugar, honey, tahini and butter stirring until creamy. Add remaining ingredients. Mix well.

Spoon rounded teaspoonfuls of dough onto cookie sheets. Bake for 10-12 minutes, or until the cookies start to turn golden brown.

Quinoa and Banana Muffins

Serves 12

Ingredients:

1 cup flour

½ cup quinoa

2 ripe bananas, mashed

¼ cup sugar

½ cup milk

1 egg

3 tbsp sunflower oil

1 tsp vanilla

1 tbsp baking powder

½ tsp cinnamon

½ tsp salt

Directions:

Preheat oven to 350 F. Combine all wet ingredients and mix well.

In a separate bowl combine dry ingredients. Add dry ingredients to wet ingredients gently stirring.

Grease or line 12 muffin tins. Spoon dough evenly into cups. Bake for 15 minutes or until a toothpick comes out clean.

Quinoa Fruit Salad

Serves 2

Ingredients:

¼ cup quinoa

1 apple, diced

2 peaches, diced

½ cup strawberries, sliced

2 tbsp honey

1 tsp cinnamon

1 tbsp lemon juice

2 tbsp chia seeds

Directions:

Wash and cook quinoa according to package directions.

Slice the fruit and layer it in a deep bowl. When the quinoa is ready and cooled, toss it in the bowl too.

Combine the lemon juice, honey and cinnamon and add it to the fruit salad. Mix very well. Serve sprinkled with chia seeds.

Chocolate Quinoa Cake

Serves 12

Ingredients:

2 cups cooked quinoa, cold

1 1/4 cups white sugar

4 eggs

3/4 cup melted butter

1/2 cup yogurt

1 cup cocoa powder

1 tbsp baking powder

1 tsp baking soda

1/2 teaspoon salt

1/2 cup chocolate chips

1/2 cup chopped walnuts

1 1/2 teaspoons vanilla extract

1 tsp rum aroma

Directions:

Preheat oven to 350 degrees F. Grease a rectangular cake pan.

Blend quinoa, butter, eggs, yogurt, vanilla extract and rum aroma together in a blender until smooth.

Combine sugar, cocoa powder, baking powder, baking soda, and salt together in a deep bowl. Stir quinoa mixture into sugar mixture until batter is well combined. Add chocolate chips and walnuts into batter.

Pour into the prepared pan and bake in the preheated oven until a toothpick inserted in the cake comes out clean, 40-45 minutes. Cool cake on a wire rack.

Quinoa Cinnamon Pancakes

Serves: 4

Ingredients:

1 cup cooked quinoa

3/4 cup flour

2 large eggs, beaten

1/4 cup milk

1 tbsp baking powder

2 tsp cinnamon

1/2 tsp salt

1 tbsp sunflower oil

1 tbsp vanilla extract

powdered sugar, to serve

Directions:

Sift flour and cinnamon into a medium bowl. Add quinoa, baking powder and salt.

In another bowl whisk together eggs, milk, vanilla and oil until smooth. Add egg mixture to flour mixture and stir to combine.

Heat a large nonstick skillet over medium to medium-low. Drop batter by heaping tablespoonfuls into the skillet and cook until bubbles appear on top, about 1-2 minutes. Flip pancakes and cook until golden brown, about 1-2 minutes.

A Few Words at the End

If you have tried some of my recipes, you probably understand why quinoa is such a wonderful food and I like it so much. Don't forget that any of these recipes can be varied and ingredients can be replaced according to your taste or what you currently have at home. I didn't include lots of meat or fish recipes because I don't eat meat often, but you can serve quinoa salads or stews as side dishes with almost all meat recipes.

Sometimes when I am cooking only for myself or when I am in a hurry I simply mix quinoa with spaghetti sauce or with a can of baked beans and have a delicious meal. Other times I can toss it with soy sauce and eat it with some diced fresh vegetables. The combinations are infinite and all depend on your personal taste.

Eating healthy foods doesn't have to be unpleasant or time consuming. Now you have a few ideas and I hope you enjoy them and have fun experimenting with this fantastic, healthy grain.

FREE BONUS INSIDE: 20 Healthy Gluten-free Superfood Smoothies for Easy and Natural Weight Loss

Mango and Asparagus Smoothie

Serves: 2

Prep time: 5 min

Ingredients:

1 frozen banana, chopped

1 cup water or green tea

1 mango, peeled and chopped

½ cup raw asparagus, chopped

1 lime, juiced

1 tsp sesame seeds

Directions:

Combine ingredients in a blender and purée until smooth. Enjoy!

.

Pineapple and Asparagus Smoothie

Serves: 2

Prep time: 5 min

Ingredients:

2-3 ice cubes

1 cup apple juice

1 pear, cut

½ cup raw asparagus, chopped

½ cup pineapple, chopped

2-3 mint leaves

Directions:

Combine ingredients in a blender and purée until smooth. Enjoy!

Fennel and Kale Smoothie

Serves: 2

Prep time: 5 min

Ingredients:

1-2 ice cubes

1 cup coconut water

1 cup fennel

2-3 kale leaves

2-3 fresh figs

2 limes, juiced

Directions:

Combine ingredients in a blender and purée until smooth. Enjoy!

Kids' Favorite Kale Smoothie

Serves: 2

Prep time: 5 min

Ingredients:

2-3 ice cubes

1½ cup apple juice

1 small apple, cut

½ cup pineapple chunks

½ cucumber, cut

3 leaves kale

Directions:

Combine ingredients in a blender and purée until smooth. Enjoy!

Kids' Favorite Spinach Smoothie

Serves: 2

Prep time: 5 min

Ingredients:

1 frozen banana

1 cup orange juice

1 apple, cut

1 cup baby spinach

1 tsp vanilla extract

Directions:

Combine ingredients in a blender and purée until smooth. Enjoy!

Paleo Mojito Smoothie

Serves: 2

Prep time: 5 min

Ingredients:

1 cup ice

1 cup coconut water, milk or plain water

1 big pear, chopped

2-3 limes, juiced, or peeled and cut

20-25 leaves fresh mint

3 dates, pitted

Directions:

Juice the limes or peel and cut them and combine with the other ingredients in a blender. Process until smooth. Enjoy!

Winter Greens Smoothie

Serves: 2

Prep time: 5 min

Ingredients:

2 broccoli florets, frozen

1½ cup coconut water

½ banana

½ cup pineapple

1 cup fresh spinach

2 kale leaves

Directions:

Combine ingredients in blender and blend until smooth. Enjoy!

Delicious Kale Smoothie

Serves: 2

Prep time: 5 min

Ingredients:

2-3 ice cubes

1½ cup apple juice

3-4 kale leaves

1 apple, cut

1 cup strawberries

½ tsp cloves

Directions:

Combine ingredients in blender and purée until smooth.

Cherry Smoothie

Serves: 2

Prep time: 5 min

Ingredients:

2-3 ice cubes

1½ cup almond or coconut milk

1½ cup pitted and frozen cherries

½ avocado

1 tsp cinnamon

1 tsp chia seeds

Directions :

Combine all ingredients into a blender and process until smooth. Enjoy!

Banana and Coconut Smoothie

Serves: 2

Prep time: 5 min

Ingredients:

1 frozen banana, chopped

1½ cup coconut water

2-3 small broccoli florets

1 tbsp coconut butter

Directions :

Add all ingredients into a blender and blend until the smoothie turns into an even and smooth consistency. Enjoy!

Avocado and Pineapple Smoothie

Serves: 2

Prep time: 5 min

Ingredients:

3-4 ice cubes

1½ cup coconut water

½ avocado

2 cups diced pineapple

Directions:

Combine all ingredients in a blender, and blend until smooth. Enjoy!

Carrot and Mango Smoothie

Serves: 2

Prep time: 5 min

Ingredients:

1 cup frozen mango chunks

1 cup carrot juice

½ cup orange juice

1 carrot, chopped

1 tsp chia seeds

1 tsp grated ginger

Directions:

Combine all ingredients in a blender, and blend until smooth. Enjoy!

Strawberry and Coconut Smoothie

Serves: 2

Prep time: 5 min

Ingredients:

3-4 ice cubes

1½ cup coconut milk

2 cups fresh strawberries

1 tsp chia seeds

Directions:

Place all ingredients in a blender and purée until smooth. Enjoy!

Beautiful Skin Smoothie

Serves: 2

Prep time: 5 min

Ingredients:

1 cup frozen strawberries

1½ cup green tea

1 peach, chopped

½ avocado

5-6 raw almonds

1 tsp coconut oil

Directions:

Place all ingredients in a blender and purée until smooth. Enjoy!

Kiwi and Pear Smoothie

Serves: 2

Prep time: 5 min

Ingredients:

1 frozen banana, chopped

3 oranges, juiced

2 kiwi, peeled and halved

1 pear, chopped

1 tbsp coconut butter

Directions:

Juice oranges and combine all ingredients in a blender then blend until smooth. Enjoy!

Tropical Smoothie

Serves: 2

Prep time: 5 min

Ingredients:

2-3 ice cubes

1½ cup coconut water

½ avocado

1 mango, peeled, diced

1 cup pineapple, chopped

2-3 dates, pitted

Directions:

Place all ingredients in a blender and purée until smooth. Enjoy!

Melon Smoothie

Serves: 2

Prep time: 5 min

Ingredients:

1 frozen banana, chopped

1-2 frozen broccoli florets

1 cup coconut water

½ honeydew melon, cut in pieces

1 tsp chia seeds

Directions:

Combine all ingredients in a blender, and blend until smooth.

Healthy Skin Smoothie

Serves: 2

Prep time: 5 min

Ingredients:

1 cup frozen berries

1 cup almond milk

½ avocado

1 pear

1 tbsp ground pumpkin seeds

1 tsp vanilla extract

Directions :

Put all ingredients in a blender and blend until smooth. Enjoy!

Paleo Dessert Smoothie

Serves: 2

Prep time: 5 min

Ingredients:

1 frozen banana

1 cup coconut water

1 cup raspberries

2 apricots, chopped

1 tbsp almond butter

Directions:

Put all ingredients into blender. Blend until smooth. Enjoy!

Easy Superfood Smoothie

Serves: 2

Prep time: 5 min

Ingredients:

3-4 ice cubes

1½ cup green tea

1 pear, chopped

½ cup blueberries

½ cup blackberries

1 tbsp almond butter

Directions :

Place all ingredients in a blender and blend for until even. Enjoy!

About the Author

Vesela lives in Bulgaria with her family of six (including the Jack Russell Terrier). Her passion is going green in everyday life and she loves to prepare homemade cosmetic and beauty products for all her family and friends.

Vesela has been publishing her cookbooks for over a year now. If you want to see other healthy family recipes that she has published, together with some natural beauty books, you can check out her Author Page on Amazon.

Printed in Great Britain
by Amazon